Ruan Milborrow is 66 years old and is also a copywriter of over 40 years standing, working mainly in London for supposed fancy advertising agencies. He's rather flukily won nearly every advertising award going during his career.
He's worked with many personalities from Paul and Linda McCartney, and Diana, Princess of Wales to Mary Portas and David Cameron.
He's best known for working mainly on fashion and music accounts, with a liberal smattering of wit and humour attached. He was strangely made Freeman of the City of London and probably accidentally included in Debrett's People of Today as a result of doing ok in his day job.
Due to some kind people telling him repeatedly over the years that he has a nice BBC-type voice, he's now also represented as a voiceover artist.
Ruan lives near Cirencester in the Cotswolds.

66... and worried!

An **A-Z** of my Anxiety
(and maybe yours?)

Ruan Milborrow

Design and illustrations
by Mark Nightingale

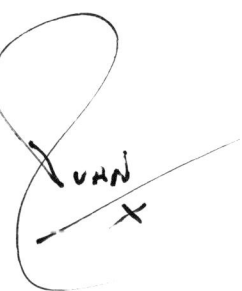

QUEEN ANNE EDITIONS

First published in Great Britain in 2025
by Queen Anne Editions.

An imprint of Queen Anne Press.

queenannepress.co.uk

1 3 5 7 9 10 8 6 4 2

Copyright © Ruan Milborrow 2025.

The right of Ruan Milborrow to be identified as the author of this work has been asserted in accordance with the Copyright, Designs and Patents Act of 1988.

All rights reserved. No part of this publication may be reproduced, stored in a retrieval system, or transmitted in any form or by any means, electronic, mechanical, photocopying, recording, or otherwise, without the prior permission of both the copyright owner and the above publisher of this book.

ISBN (Paperback) 9780993160936

ISBN (eBook) 9780993160943

Designed and illustrated by Mark Nightingale.

Typeset in 12/16 point Fournier on 115gsm coated paper.

Printed by TJ Books, Padstow, Cornwall.

Dedicated to the late Dr Raghu Gaind,
who undoubtedly saved me

... and to Debbie and Thomas.
I love you.

is for introduction

This little book is all about my anxiety. What makes me anxious and how I deal with it. It's not a self-help book, but I do hope you find some sort of comfort from it.

I don't 'suffer' from anxiety. I live with it. Constantly. It's part of me. It's not going to go away. It's what makes me me. It's not my friend, but it's always by my side. I wake up with anxiety. I go to sleep with anxiety. If I didn't feel anxious, I'd be worried.

Winston Churchill called his anxiety and depression 'his black dog' – his faithful companion. I know exactly what he meant. So, forgive me if I mention my similar experiences of it once or twice throughout my ramblings.

Anyway, I digress – I even manage to hide my anxiety from my family and my friends. Maybe they know it's there. But they're all far too polite to mention it. I've tried to be as honest as I can writing this, but I do realise it might come across that I'm just a little bit odd. I'm not. I'm just an average, anxious 66-year-old chap who wants to get on with life as best as possible under the circumstances in a quiet, unassuming and kind way.

I realise that I've stuck my head above the parapet in writing this. But if you're aiming to take a pot-shot at me, please miss.

is for anxiety

It first struck when I was about 13. I was caught cheating in a maths test at school. I was copying the answers from the boy next to me. Can't remember his name. Mr Spielman, the teacher spotted me. He shouted at me and gave me a detention. I immediately broke out in a very cold sweat.

All these years later, I can recognise it as my first panic attack. What he didn't realise was that my eyesight was so bad that I couldn't read the questions on the blackboard. I had no choice but to copy the answers from my chum.

Was this incident responsible for a life of constant anxiety? I don't know. What do you think? Has anything like this happened to you?

is also for age

In my head I'm 16, nearly 17. In reality, I'm 66. Also, in my head, I can't drive. I don't own a home. I'm not married. I don't have a job. I spend all my money on records and music magazines. So, I now live in this teenage-like state where I imagine that the day-to-day problems of being an adult don't exist.

The world seems a lot safer and a lot more pleasant this way. Ok, I have to drift back into adulthood every now and again – to pay the bills, to try and be an attentive husband and stepfather, to hold down a job.

But escaping from reality and the pressures of everyday life in my head is a great way to keep anxiety at bay. You should try it sometime. I recommend it.

is also for acting

If you have anxiety, you'll need to be a good actor. You have to be to live your life. Over the years I've learned to keep my anxiety to myself and not to burden other people with it. I believe only three or four people know what I have to live with. Constantly. Even then, they can't know exactly what it's like.

I've lost count of the hundreds of times I've been told off for going to bed too early, getting up too late or staring into space. What other people don't see is the total feeling of despair within. However, I try my best to function and pretend, or act, as if there's nothing wrong. I do that at home, at work and when I'm out and about. There are two Ruans – the one that's sociable, cheery and hopefully, kind, And the one that's the complete opposite, who finds every day a struggle and just wants to disappear.

So, if you're anything like me – keep going, smile sweetly and do your best. Like many really accomplished actors, you may find that you completely lose yourself in the role you're playing – and then your anxiety will disappear, albeit temporarily. One thing you must never forget, take a bow and give yourself a round of applause at the end of every day. You're a star!

is also for Adidas

When I was 14, I was so into playing football that it was quite frankly, embarrassing.
My parents sent me to a good school and I completely wasted my education, academically. All I could think about was music (more of that later) and playing football. I wasn't any good but wasn't bad (Just like most things in my life. See 'imposter', also later on).

Anyway, my prize possession was a scruffy, second-hand pair of black and white Adidas Samba football trainers that my friend Simon Sharp gave me, or he might have sold them to me for 50p, I can't really remember. He considered them to be worn out, which they were, but I wore them and felt I was a footballing star. Which I clearly wasn't. I think they were so worn that they had a hole in the sole, but I didn't care. They had a long tongue that flipped down –

so cool. I could never have afforded a new pair. I felt good wearing those shoes, which is where I'm getting to in this story.

Now, fifty years later, I decided to buy myself a pair of brand-new Adidas Sambas. Yes, they still make them and they're identical to those of my schooldays. I bought them online and they arrived in a couple of days – oh, how times have changed. And guess what? They are the most comfortable shoes I have ever owned.

I wear them all the time, no matter what else I'm wearing – they go with everything. I've even been told that they're 'cool' by my frighteningly much younger friends at work.

So, the point is to help keep anxiety in its box, stick with what you know and are used to.
 Going rogue can cause stress: 'familiar' is the important word here. It provides comfort and reassurance. Even if it means going back in time, 50 years or so to achieve it.

is also for attention span

As I get older, I find it more difficult to concentrate – my attention span is much shorter these days. Why is this, I wonder? Am I now getting the onset of dementia? It's always not far from my mind. Watching television is when it pops up quite often. I find it hard to follow the plot of sometimes even quite easy-peasy programmes, like Father Brown or Grantchester.

I tend to get quite a lot of light-hearted stick about this from my family, who accuse me of not concentrating and drifting off. Some might call this brain fog. But what no-one really knows that while I'm watching TV, my mind is racing. It's full of angst and worry. The anxiety is taking up so much space in my head that it's completely excommunicating Father Brown, if you get my drift?

By the way, one of the reasons that I'm writing a book like this is that my story is made up of lots of bite-sized chunks. My anxiety wouldn't let me write a continuous narrative, Hopefully, if you're anything like me, it will help my story easier to read too. You can dip in and dip out of it, you can read any bits you like – rather like a dictionary. You can even read it backwards. If I were you, I'd keep this little book by the loo. You can lock the door for a few precious minutes, read a bit and then unlock the door knowing it's not just you that faces a life of constant anxiety, but it actually happens to quite a lot of people.

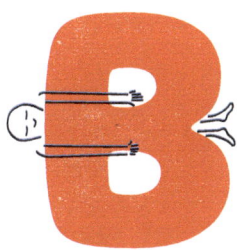

is for bed

I cannot tell you how much I love my bed. It's where I feel safe. It's my sanctuary from the pressures of the outside world. It's where I can relax, it's where I think and it's where I sleep. Most importantly, it's where I go when I feel any kind of anxiety creeping up on me. If I have a fault (and I'm the first to admit that I have many), it's that I spend far too much time in bed. But for me, it's the perfect way to keep anxiety at arm's length.

If you feel a bit jittery, go to bed, close your eyes and imagine all is right with the world. If you can get a loved one, relative or friend to bring you a cup of tea, then that will be sheer heaven. I find Radio 4 and The Archers helps too. Put simply, there's nothing like snuggling under the sheets, with a cosy blanket on top and shutting yourself away until all is right again. And believe me, it will be right again.

is also for birthday

You must always celebrate your birthday. It needn't be a lavish celebration. It could be a slice of Victoria sponge with your best friend, a pint down your local Spoons with your mates or some takeaway fish 'n' chips with a loved one.

The point is you are a year older and a year wiser. You've made it. Life is hard, so celebrate another year and congratulate yourself for all you're worth.

is also for biscuits

As you delve further on into my ramblings, you'll find out how a restorative cup of tea really helps me when mild anxiety pops up. But when a cuppa is combined with a couple (or whole pack!) of biscuits, then the world does feel more than a tad rosier.

However, they do have to be certain types of biscuits. Posh ones are definitely not my cup of tea. I do hope you agree with my choice, but they have to be either Bourbons, Custard Creams, Fig Rolls, Jammie Dodgers or, my only concession to the modern world, Jaffa Cakes. My wife calls them my 'war biscuits' because they're so old and, to her, simply frightful.

But to me, it's probably another way of me looking back to my childhood with the comforting food I was brought up on. It's yet again, the familiar helping me to calm down. I know it sounds daft but it works for me, so go on, give it a try. By the way, I still can't believe you can buy a whole pack of Fig Rolls in Tesco for just 49p!

However, there is a down side – when I start, I just can't stop. I can easily munch through a whole pack of Jaffa Cakes in one sitting. Crumbs!...

is also for breathe

I know it sounds a bit daft, but when anxiety pays you an unwelcome visit, try not to forget to breathe. Not breathing can do us all harm! I've got this real habit of holding my breath. I don't know I'm doing it. I also breathe through my mouth and not my nose, which doesn't really help. It might even contribute to me being anxious all the time? It's only writing this that makes me think that might be the case. What do you reckon?

Anyway, deep breaths through the nose, holding for a few seconds and then breathing slowly out through your mouth can really help. It calms everything down. I'm doing it now and everything seems to slow down, so it becomes much easier to think straight. I don't do this enough. So, promise me you'll give it a go.

Now, one thing I'm slightly embarrassed to tell you – it's a bit yucky, even disgusting – is that when I get stressed I retch and cough, and for all the tea in China, I can't stop myself from doing it. It normally happens in the bathroom at the beginning of the day. It's a fear of what the day may have in store for me. It can also happen at other times though; I had a creative meeting yesterday with some people that I had never met before. I kept it together and the meeting went well. But as soon as I got back to the sanctuary of my car. I started to retch uncontrollably. Then, I remembered to take deep breaths and things soon started to calm down again. I'm never actually sick.

But, crikey, the noise is horrible and it's definitely not doing me any good. This has been happening to me for years, and I'm led to believe it's quite common, so don't worry if it happens to you too. It's like having mini panic attacks. They won't last long. To me, however, they are quite debilitating, and the act of retching is like the black dog of anxiety barking out loud and saying to me, 'I'm still here you know'...

is for change

Now this is a tricky subject. Later on, I talk about how I seek comfort from the familiar. But – and I find this really difficult to write – change is good. Now, I'm at my most anxious when my routine is disrupted. I get panicky, I feel sick, I start to sweat, and I have to flee wherever I'm at. But what if it's more than just a simple change in routine? What if it's ending a relationship, starting a new job, going somewhere new on holiday or moving house? Change of this kind means uncertainty.

Uncertainty, to me, means things being out of my control. This is huge. It literally makes me feel hopelessly unwell. I cannot cope and I usually take to my bed.

But, and this is the weird bit, I do believe change is good.

We only get one relatively short life, so we should make the most of it – experience something new. So, if you can hack it, push yourself and give yourself a huge pat on the back when you achieved a significant change in your life. However, I'm a cowardy custard – change is not for me. Rather sadly, almost more than anything else, it's really held me back in life. Please don't let it happen to you...

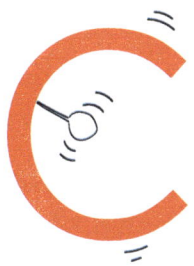

is also for church bells

Hmm... you may find this a bit random. But I'm lucky enough to live close to a church and every Thursday evening, from 7pm-9pm, the bell ringers practise their skills. So, I go to bed early, open the bedroom window and listen to the sound of the church bells. They're glorious and they for some reason, literally resonate with me. In my head, it's like something out of a Miss Marple mystery. To me, their sound personifies English village life.

Most importantly though, they relax me, my anxiety subsides, and I can drift off to sleep. Sound is so effective as a suppressor of anxiety. For some people it's the sound of the sea, whales calling each other, rainwater or merely the spoken word.

When I lived on my own in London, I had a clock radio – I used to listen to Radio 4 when I went to bed and the radio would turn itself off after an hour. I never heard it switch off because by then I would be fast asleep. So, my advice to you is to find a sound that allows you to relax and happily drift off… ring any bells?

P.S: I'm going to get a tad bossy here – if you really want a good night's sleep don't look at your phone or tablet whilst in bed. They make your brain overactive and you will not be able to quickly go to sleep. It's difficult, I know, I learned the hard way…

is also for cheery

I touched upon this elsewhere... there are two Ruans – the cheery one and the one wracked with despair. I've read a lot about how many comedians are severely burdened with a lack of confidence, total depression and debilitating sadness. In their profession they have to be seen to be funny. I feel like a bit of a comedian myself in trying to keep this together. Or should I say, double act.

is also for chocolate

Chocolate, rather like tea, has magical powers. Now, I'm telling you what works for me, but why don't you give it a go? ... you never know.

I tend to keep a bar of chocolate by my bed. To be precise, it's Lindt Lindor Milk, the bar in the red pack. Oh, it has a lovely creamy, soothing milky taste that washes over me and relaxes me in readiness for the long night ahead. (Perhaps, Mr Lindt might want to send a few bars my way for plugging his product. I'd be most grateful!)

When I feel anxiety creeping up on me, and I use the word 'creeping' deliberately because it often feels like a naughty black dog that is trying to sneak onto my bed without me noticing it – I have just one square of chocolate to settle me down for the night. Now, I have to confess this works for anxiety lite, not the full fat version. For that I suggest you turn to my 'L is for lists' entry.

Incidentally, my idea of sheer heaven takes place every December when I'm usually given a chocolate Advent calendar! I tend to sleep well that month. It's strange, but a treat of one square of chocolate definitely affects my brain in a slightly soporific way, it makes me a bit sleepy. I guess that's why lots of people have a cup of hot chocolate before they retire for the night.

Another reason for my indulgence is that to me, it's a little reward for making it through the last 24 hours. I got there and I have to do it all again tomorrow. However, as long as there is a bar of delicious milky choccy within arm's reach, I feel I can tackle the onslaughts of the day ahead.

is also for collecting

I love collecting things. Now, this really is a double-edged sword. Surrounding yourself with stuff can be very comforting. It can also be very suffocating. I collect modern first editions, art, guitars, cars, pottery, orders of service, badges, magazines, CDs, DVDs – and that's just for starters. How sad is that? What do I get from it? I tell you what I get from it – anxiety!

But where would I be without all this junk or, more importantly, who would I be without it? I think it's got a lot to do with self-worth and bought contentedness. My advice to you, but, rather despairingly, not to myself, is travel light. Don't be dragged down by possessions.

After all you can't take them with you.

What you own does not define you. Concentrate on friends, loved ones, relatives, pets or whoever you feel closest to, even if it's just yourself. Declutter your environment and declutter your mind. No-one cares if you've got the latest remix of Pink Floyd's Wish You Were Here on all formats. No-one except me, sadly.

is also for comics

If you're around my age, you'll remember The Beano, The Dandy, Victor, Hotspur, TV Century 21, Whizzer & Chips, Topper, Cor!, Shoot! and a whole host of other wonderful publications. What's this got to do with anxiety, I hear you say? Well, reading these comics when I was a child made me so happy. I loved Lord

Snooty and His Pals, The Bash Street Kids, Alf Tupper – the tough of the track, Minnie the Minx, Desperate Dan and Biffo the Bear – they were my friends. It was at a time before I ever knew the meaning of anxiety. I lived in a world without responsibility.

The highlight of my year was when we used to go on our summer holidays to Eastbourne and my mum used to buy me the Summer Specials, expanded editions of my favourite comics.
I used to walk along the Promenade – my dad would buy the Daily Mirror and if I was lucky, I'd get a Beano Summer Special. Every now and again, comics would give away free gifts with an issue – usually a whoopee cushion or a brown paper sort of cone that would make a loud bang when you waved it in the air. These just blew my mind. So, what am I getting to here?... When I'm struck with anxiety, I try and think of something that made me really happy, a memory that no-one could take away from me. What's your favourite memory?

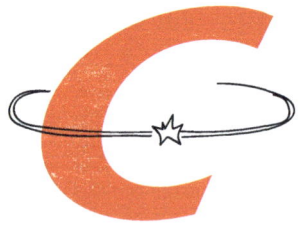

is also for confidence

I'm completely bereft of confidence. I think this is as a result of being so anxious all the time. A few things have happened in my life that have completely knocked me for six. They're usually things that have been said to me that have had a devastating impact on my self-confidence. I think having anxiety makes you over-think almost everything to a degree bordering on complete ridiculousness.

I often wonder what it must be like to just breeze through life without a care in the world. Bit silly really, because it will never apply to me. Anxiety also leads to an almost constant feeling of paranoia. I constantly worry about what people think of me. I'm sure they reckon that I'm weird, strange, odd and probably not very nice, and a tad rude at times. Really, I just want to tell them that I am nice, but just a bit frightened by life and this is what makes me not be like them. Anxiety leads to over sensitivity in a major way. I am not being stand offish, aloof, moody or whatever. I just have zero self-esteem, zero confidence and zero self-belief. Please, please tell me it's quite common…

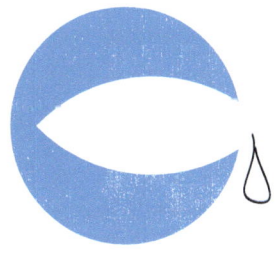

is also for crying

Yes, the sad truth is that I'm a bit of a cry baby. Actually 'bit' is an understatement, I spend most of life about to cry. It's odd, but since my anxiety started to spiral a few years back, I can now burst into tears at the drop of a hat. Sad films bring me out in floods; happy films, the same. Puppies, babies, in-love couples, ringing church bells, kind words, harsh words – they all have the same effect – I start sobbing, almost uncontrollably. But do you know what? I don't mind at all. I'm not embarrassed by it. I believe that my sensitive side has emerged from years of repression. In fact, I wish I could cry more. 'What?' I hear you say. You see, when

I cry, I feel a great sense of release and the anxiety leaves my body.

Sometimes, rather ironically, when I want to have a good sob, it won't come. It, rather like the black dog itself, creeps up on me when I am least expecting it. For example, I asked my son the other day what his favourite restaurant was. I was expecting him to say The Wolseley, Manoir aux Quat' Saisons or somewhere fancy like that. But he actually said it was 'eating a crab sandwich on St Mawes harbour with you'. Well, that was it, the tears were rolling down my cheeks like a waterfall. It was difficult to say whether these were tears of sadness or joy, but it got to me none the less.

I may be a complete softie, but I do recommend to you when the going gets a tad tough, don't be afraid to let it out with a good weep. You'll feel a lot better, I promise you.

is also for cuddle

When someone puts their arm around me, gives me a hug or gives me a cuddle, I literally feel the anxiety fleeing from my body. I then don't feel alone. I feel that someone cares.

To me, when I'm having a bad day, a cuddle is worth more than I could ever say. So, don't be afraid to return the favour. If you spot a friend or family member in need of some kind of support, put your arm around them and tell them it's going to be alright.

Oh, and I should say, when someone gives me a cuddle, I often cry. But don't worry, they are tears of joy, not sadness…

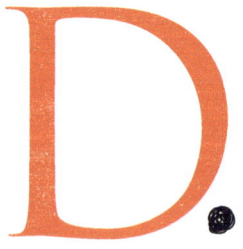

is for death

I hope you're enjoying reading my ramblings and I so hope you make it to the end. But if I had to say what the true essence of what this book is about, and I don't want to alarm you, but I have to say it would be about dying.

I've a morbid fear of death and dying. Now this may be an age thing – I'll leave it up to you to decide. But assuming you are roughly the same age as me, I'd love to know if it too strikes a chord with you.

Now, as you read on you'll learn how crippling my anxiety is, but at the same time I hope I put across how much I love life. The thing is, I just don't want to leave the party early. Enough of that – let's be a little more positive, shall we?

is also for denim

Ok, this may be a little odd, but it may resonate in some way with you. In my early years I always struggled with my image – the way I looked, more specifically, the way I dressed. I was so desperate to blend in, be accepted by others and fundamentally, not look stupid or be thought of as weird. How I was perceived by the world made me anxious. And truth be told, it still does.

I went through a hippie stage – Afghan coat, loons, patchouli oil etc; a smart Sloane Ranger/preppy/yuppie stage – Husky or Barbour jacket, moleskin trousers, checked shirts, Gucci shoes, etc; a scruffy stage – oversized T-shirts, battered jeans, trainers that were falling apart, etc. I even went through a very embarrassing sort of TV star stage – I remember watching The Return of the Saint and The Persuaders thinking I wanted to look like Lord Brett Sinclair or Simon Templar, both played by Roger Moore.

I even went and bought a pair of trousers from a very posh gentlemen's outfitters in Jermyn Street, because it was credited at the end of The Saint. What was I thinking? Why didn't someone tell me I was being a bit of a twit?

Anyway, to cut a long story short, another of my manic dress phases was wearing Ralph Lauren because whilst at agricultural college, I really got into polo. Yes, I know, very la-di-da. And, goodness me, blow me down, after a brief flirtation with Ben Sherman, that stuck. So, all those years later, I have learned to overcome my anxiety when it comes to putting on my clothes every morning. I always wear a Ralph Lauren shirt, usually a denim one. I think I have eight identical denim shirts. One for every day of the week and one spare. In fact, whenever I go into a Ralph Lauren store, I always come out with an identical denim shirt. It's sort of comforting. I always wear either Levi jeans or M&S blue trousers. I wear M&S boxers and socks. A Ralph Lauren woolly scarf to hide behind. And now, mostly, Adidas trainers.

I think I was doing the daily-wear-the-same look long before Steve Jobs and Mark Zuckerberg. The serious point is that I don't have to angst anymore at what to wear. I am yet again, comfortable with the familiar. So, find a look that reflects who you are, stick with it and it'll be one less thing to worry about.

is also for Denmark Street

For those who have never heard of it, Denmark Street is in the west end of London. It's a sort of grubby and dingy short street, just off the Charing Cross Road – it's also known as Tin Pan Alley. It's a street where dreams can come true.

One tried and trusted way to forget about my anxiety in my youth was to gaze lovingly at the electric guitars in the windows of the many musical instrument shops that lined the street and imagine I was in a rock band.

I had no money at the time and used to go into the shops and ask, if not plead, for the latest Fender or Gibson catalogues. I can still remember the distinctive smell of the print in these catalogues. I must have been 14 or 15 at the time and regularly got a cheap day return on the Tube from home to Tottenham Court Road merely to look at the wonderous guitars on display. I can still remember the shop names – Selmer, Orange, Fender Soundhouse, Rose Morris, Top Gear, Macari's...

But why am I telling you this? Fifty years on, I still get the same thrill when I go back and look at the guitars. I will still make a point of going to Denmark Street when things aren't great and look at the guitars. It's like going back in time. I found something I truly loved and was passionate about. It took my mind away from the despair I felt so often. It was pure escapism. It gave me the chance to dream. So, try and find something that enables you to take a well-deserved break from your darker moments. It really does work – but I still can't play the guitar.

is also for depression

This is an interesting one, that I haven't really sorted out in my mind, to tell you the truth. I wonder what you'll think. Do I get depressed as well as anxious? There's no doubt in my mind that depression and anxiety are very closely related – they are like brother and sister. My anxiety is truly crippling. I feel a sense of hopelessness and fear almost every minute of every day. But rather oddly, I still love life. I'm rarely what you'd call, 'fed up'. I always imagine depression to be a feeling of not being able to get out bed in the morning, not being able to keep going and wanting it all to end. I'm only talking about what I feel. I'm no expert and the scientific explanation is something that is beyond my pea-like brain.

But I'll tell you something that may make you cross. And if it does, I completely understand – I wouldn't change a thing about myself. Yes, ok,

looking like George Clooney or Harry Styles may have its advantages… My anxiety is part of me. I have lived with it for most of my life.
It's not going to go away. So, I'm stuck with it. But I wouldn't have it any other way.

I have another fear. And that is a fear of being average, being normal. I gain comfort from being different. I look at the world differently. I work in a creative industry where we have to produce work that, I suppose, has to be out of the ordinary in order to gain stand out and attention. I'm sure this is why so many so-called creative people are beset with issues and problems. So, if you have anxiety, remember you are different and really rather special. Unique, one might say…

is also for dreams

To escape the absolute stomach knot-tightening feeling of dread that anxiety brings on, I tend to go to bed very early, too early one might say.

I find evenings more difficult than daytime. The darkness of the night tends to make me more circumspect and alone with my thoughts. So, now I take to my bed at a ridiculously early hour. If I'm feeling bad, this is usually around 7 o'clock. Just in time for The Archers. I take a hot water bottle up with me and this adds to snugness I feel when I disappear from the world under the duvet. I listen to The Archers, maybe a podcast or two.

My lovely wife will bring me up a cup of tea around 8 and then I will quickly succumb to sleep and that will be the end of the day. Now, 'What has that got to do with dreams?' I hear you say...

Well, because I go to bed when I'm not really tired, I don't tend to fall into a deep sleep. In fact, even the slightest noise will awaken me from my slumbers. But because I'm not in a deep sleep, I tend to dream more. And the awful upshot of this is although I've dropped off, my anxiety hasn't really left me. It's then I start to dream, and they are frighteningly awful. There are recurring themes. I'm often trying to get somewhere but failing. I'm usually travelling by Tube, but never getting on the right train, getting lost in the underground maze of the station, coming out at stations that I've never heard of. Or I'm desperately trying to make phone calls on my mobile but cannot get a signal, or have trouble in repeatedly dialling the number correctly. Another common theme is that I've arranged to meet someone, but get horribly lost in walking there, even though I supposedly know the streets well. In short, my dreams are about failing to do a simple task.

Now, I take this as a sign of my failure in life. They make me feel wretched and the only good thing is that when I wake up, I realise that they are not actually real and I feel an overwhelming sense of relief. I know what you're going to say, why don't you go to bed later? The thing is I find, night time and darkness really hard.

I have difficulty concentrating on the television, I often feel cold, and despair seems to flood over me like a cold shower when I sit down of an evening with time to think which is when it all starts to go awry. The only answer is retreat to bed. Will this situation improve? In my dreams.

is also for driving

Since I was a little boy, I've always liked cars. As a treat, my dad used to buy me Autocar or Motor magazine. I collected model cars and had hundreds. I still have a few Corgi Toys, in their boxes, which I cherish today as a reminder of happy times past. I have the James Bond Aston Martin DB5, Batmobile, the Toyota from You Only Live Twice, The Man from U.N.C.L.E. Oldsmobile and The Saint's Volvo amongst a few others. Just thinking about it as I write, they are my favourite possessions, as they remind me of a happy childhood with my mum and my dad.

Anyway, I digress. No matter how anxious I may be, and at times, as you already know, it can be pretty overwhelming, I can still safely and enjoyably drive a car. In fact, especially when I am on my own, I can spend hours driving. I put the heater on full, no matter what the weather is outside, tune the radio to Radio 4, maybe have some sweets in the glovebox and drive off. Now the interesting thing is that I absolutely hate being a passenger in a car. I get full blown anxiety, my whole body goes stiff, and I convince myself that I am about to die in a horrible crash. I hyperventilate, cannot talk and feel my heart race. I cannot tell you how awful I feel. Now, what does that tell you?

I reckon it's all about being in control. When I'm driving myself, I'm in control in a bubble, a cocoon of sorts, protected from outside life. My world and its problems are outside the car.

As an aside, I was listening to Gyles Brandreth's excellent podcast called Rosebud, and he has exactly the same experiences whenever he is driven anywhere. Is it an age thing, I wonder? I do think it's about control, coupled with a fear of death which is growing more every day that I live. However, when I look back, even as a child, I didn't like to be a passenger and was often car sick. My mum used to dose me up on some ghastly tablets called Kwells whenever we'd go out in my dad's Rover 2000. Is that what's driving my anxiety? I'd love to find out the truth one day – it may help.

is for EOG

I'm afraid to tell you that as well as living on the emotional rollercoaster that my anxiety brings, I also now have to live daily with EOG. Oh, no... 'What's EOG?' I hear you say... Well, to give EOG its full name, it's Early Onset Grumpiness. Yes, I find myself, I believe as a result of my anxiety, now grumpy most of time. I have reconciled myself to this, but for others around me it's no laughing matter and it has a profound effect on them. The symptoms of EOG include shouting at the television, complaining about the cost of everything, criticising the competence of other drivers and not wanting to go to garden centres – basically it's me being a bit of a pain all round.

Here's the big thing, I jest – I'm not really grumpy at all – people think I am, especially when they first meet me. The truth is my anxiety gets hold of me so strongly that I often panic and appear bad-tempered. I'm not, I promise you.

I'm just in a real tizzy. Am I alone in this? Is it something you recognise in your life? What can we do about it?

is also for Eric

Eric Clapton has played such a major part in my life, so I'm afraid that I'm going to waffle on about him quite a bit. When I was about 14, I decided, almost overnight, that I wanted to learn how to play the guitar. I still have no idea what actually prompted this yearning. I told my rather shocked and disbelieving dad, and he kindly bought me an Eko Ranger 6-string acoustic guitar that cost £34 from a music shop in Ilford Market.

My school chum Nicholas Ind and I then signed up for lessons at night school in nearby Loughton. There were about 30 of us in the class (including quite a few nuns, for some reason) and the sound of us all trying to play a rather ropey A chord simultaneously was simply awful.

Anyway, I digress – I heard an older boy, Rizwan Razaq, at school playing the album 461 Ocean Boulevard. I was immediately in heaven. The sounds coming out of his 6th form study were spellbinding. I had never heard anything like it. I bought the album from my local record shop, Pop Inn in South Woodford for £1.99 and it was the best investment I've ever made.
I'm listening to the album now as I am writing this and it is lifting my mood, almost like magic. I played the album over and over again. When the house music competition came around at school, I played 'Please Be With Me' from the album on my trusty acoustic guitar with a couple of housemates in the 'Contemporary Music' category and we came first!

I then bought all of Eric's albums and played them relentlessly. I first saw him play live in 1976 at the Crystal Palace Bowl. I went on my own and I still remember it like it was yesterday. It changed my life. I now must have seen him play live getting on for 100 times. I have a collection of 'Eric Clapton' signed guitars that I absolutely cherish. I've met him only once – I was in Cordings, a gentlemen's country clothing store in Piccadilly, when I heard this voice behind me and I immediately recognised it as Eric. We chatted and I told him that I had just returned from New York where I had attended his charity guitar auction at Christie's. He asked if I bought a guitar and I sadly had to tell him that although I had saved up for months all I could have afforded was a guitar strap (It still went for many thousands of pounds). He sympathised and signed my business card, and we went our separate ways. But I had actually talked to my lifelong hero! I then went the same day and bought a 1969 Gibson Byrdland from Andy's guitar shop in Denmark Street to celebrate the occasion. 'But what has this got to do with anxiety?' I hear you ask?

Well, there are two things that spring to mind. One, Eric is human and like us all, he's had to deal with all sorts of horrible stuff in his life – drug addiction, alcoholism, the loss of a child, marriage break-up and probably a lot more. And there he is, still soldiering on making great music. If he can keep going after all he's been through then so can I. He's my hero. He's my role model and when I play his music or see him live, my spirits soar, and things don't seem quite so bad after all. Secondly, it was he who really nurtured my love for playing the guitar. As I've already mentioned, I'm useless at it, but I can lose myself in the moment when I pick up my battered Strat (which is also signed by Eric). My anxiety just melts away. So, my advice is having a hero or heroes to look up to is a good thing. Your hero could come from any walk of life – writer, actor, musician, comedian, chef – then try and relax and lose yourself in their writing acting, music or cooking. Focusing on that will help push your anxiety into the background. And remember they are no different to you, they will all have their problems that they have to confront. Again, it's a case of you're not alone… Finally, thank you from the bottom of my heart, Eric. Without you, things would be a lot worse…

is for familiar

The sad truth is that I constantly live in fear of anything new – new people, new places, new things… I perpetually seek comfort in the familiar. Show me anything that I'm not used to, and I

panic, I come out in a sweat and some people think I get grumpy and even a tad rude.
But it's just a high state of anxiety coming out. It's not difficult to see how edgy I am. I also usually have an overwhelming desire to run away, which I frequently do. I really try and push myself and occasionally it works. I find somewhere, somebody or something I like. But this is the exception to the rule.

I could never drive a car abroad, for example. By the way, whilst on the subject, I have an awful sense of direction – I get lost very easily. I often forget where I've parked the car. I put this down to concentrating so hard on the road ahead, that I don't actually look at the surroundings of where I am. Sound familiar to you? Just before, I wrote this, I was out and about and my wife wanted to visit a new place for a drink. This sent me into a bit of a spin and I really didn't want to go. However, we went and I was really uncomfortable and wanted to go home. I went and tried,
but in the end the café visit was just not my cup of tea.

is also for fear

This is a bit of a serious one for me... I believe a large part of my anxiety is born out of fear. I have two main fears. One is death and I have talked about that one already. Although just to add to it for a moment, I know I will die sometime. We all will. It's the process of dying that frightens me – will it be painful? How much of it will I know? What will be the effect on my wife and stepson? I still think about this daily, if I'm honest. And it really has a profound mental and physical effect on me. I find it difficult to cope with – I only have to get a head ache and I'm convinced that I have a brain tumour.

My other fear is money. I think this may be quite common in people of our age. I was stupid enough not to stash a lot away during my career towards a pension. I never was paid pop star money, so I needed what I earned. So now I'm sitting here writing this thinking I will lose my house, and I'll end up destitute and on the streets. I'm 66, I don't know how many years I've got left and not being able to provide for my wife and stepson really frightens me. Again, I live in fear of this on a daily basis. Now, in my more rational moments I know I live in a small house that's paid for, I get my state pension, and I don't live a rock 'n' roll lifestyle (I wish I did though!) So, I should be ok.

But perhaps the most debilitating thing about my anxiety is that a lot of my thoughts are totally irrational and in the cold light of day, make no sense at all. How do I get over this? Well, I constantly seek reassurance from my loved ones. I know it must really get them down, but I literally cannot help it. Yet, in writing this, I believe I am not alone in my woes… It is quite common, isn't it?

is also for food

When I've too much on my plate, food is a real help. However, most people when they get anxious lose their appetite. Well, it's the complete opposite for me. When anxiety decides to appear, I have to eat. However, I've such a complex relationship with food, that it's both my friend and my enemy. One of the reasons I'm anxious, I reckon, is because I'm fat, no, obese. That makes me very sad. I hate the way I look. I'm embarrassed about my appearance when in the company of others. I'm not attractive to the opposite sex. As far as I'm concerned, all that stuff disappeared years ago. I used to be slim. Now, I can't walk far. I get tired easily.

Ironically, I'm at my most relaxed when I'm in a restaurant. I love to eat and chat with friends. Being cooked for is such a treat and privilege. And there's no washing up. It doesn't have to be posh though. Would you like to know my top 5 eateries? I love lists, so here they are: Wagamama, Rick Stein's Seafood Restaurant in Padstow, Mr Taro's in Soho, The Hidden Hut in Portscatho and, the best of all, my kitchen at home. So, what's my advice to you regarding food? Well, enjoy it. I've had my best conversations with friends and loved ones whilst eating. Good company and great food are a brilliant combination. Troubles can be shared and even solved over a good cheese board.

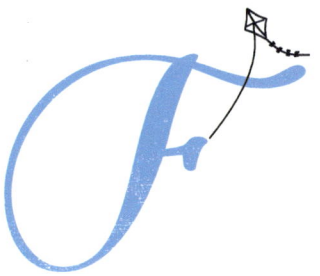

is also for fresh air

Now I've only just learned this and it's a complete revelation. I've always read that exercise is good for anxiety, but because sometimes I'm a bit daft, I never actually believed it. I'm overweight and to be truthful, quite lazy. The thought of jogging gets me reaching for the biscuit tin. But, let me tell you it really, really works. I was up until recently working in a stressful corporate environment that wasn't doing my mental health any good at all. Then, for some reason, an equally stressed-out colleague and I decided to go for a walk in Cirencester Park one lunchtime. That was it. I was converted and immediately addicted. Not only did I feel better in my head, but, just after a few lunchtime strolls, I felt fitter.

Now, you have to believe me when I say exercise and me were not great friends, but that's in the past now. You don't have to walk far nor fast to feel the effect and if you can go with a friend all the better. You can chat along the way, and you'll be surprised how far you've gone. Sometimes, rather like a computer we have to switch ourselves off and then switch ourselves on again. Well, walking allows me to switch off. And when I switch myself back on again, I feel much better for it.

I have a wonderful GP who once said to me, '10,000 steps a day? Who's got time for that?' He's right, we all lead busy lives, but just getting out for a few minutes can do the trick. But why does it work so well? Breathing in fresh air, after being in a stuffy office all morning, is what I can only describe as a natural high, I'm reliably told it releases endorphins that just make us feel good.

It's also a great distraction from having anxious thoughts. It gave me a feeling of accomplishment which was good for my self-esteem. And at the end of the day, it improved my quality of sleep. I won't be purchasing any Lycra clothing in the near future, but in a small way it changed my life for the better. Face it, we all just need to get out more…

is for garden

Again, a bit like exercise, I never knew the power of gardens, gardening and green spaces until comparatively late on in life. Now, I'm fortunate to have a garden, not a large one, but I can sit out and enjoy it when the sun shines. I don't have green fingers and can't really garden. But I'm happy to do a bit of pruning (under supervision) and I enjoy filling the green bin with cuttings, leaves, etc. My wife is a keen gardener and jolly good at it too. But, in my own little way, I am gradually learning about plants. I now know what a Box hedge is or can spot a *Verbena bonariensis* from a distance (Impressed?).

However, whilst being of no real use, I really do appreciate my garden. Sitting out there, especially with a cup of tea on a fine summer's day, is very therapeutic and relaxing. My anxiety seems to wither when sitting outside and admiring my surroundings.

Now, if you don't have a garden, I urge you to start a window box or get some houseplants. Being close to oxygenating plants, no matter how small, will have an effect on your mood. For me, the scent of some plants is quite intoxicating. Lavender, for example, has a calming, comforting and soothing effect on me. Roses, the same. Also, plants, both inside and outside the house, can help purify the air. Making it easier to breathe correctly. Apparently, being around plants can help your blood pressure too! Maybe become a member of the National Trust? We've had some great days out at their various houses and gardens. I do hope I've planted a seed of thought in your mind... I promise you it will help. Remember, sometimes life isn't a bed of roses...

is also for going out

For me, going out has always been a tad tricky. It usually results in a right old hoo-hah and is generally quite fraught. Don't get me wrong, I like going out, I really do, but it really is quite a faff. Firstly, I get so nervous. I start coughing and retching at the thought of it, especially if it's somewhere I haven't been before. So that's not a great start, is it? Also, it's usually me that does the driving and that's another problem – I have a dreadful sense of direction and lack of spatial awareness. I get lost all the time. I get really panicky and, some might say, a bit of a grumpy guts. So many times, I've parked my car and forgotten where it is. I think it's because I am so anxious about getting to where I'm going, I can't take in where I actually am – yes, it's even a bit confusing to explain. Then, it gets even worse!

Listen to this. When I get panicky, I need to go to the loo – urgently, very urgently. No, it's not an age thing, before you ask. I've always been like it. I recently went to a park with a friend that I hadn't visited before. Suddenly I was overcome with panic and desperately needed to find a toilet. A totally embarrassing accident was avoided by mere seconds. This really has restricted me in life. I call it 'bookshop disease', as it always seems to occur whenever I go into a bookshop.

So, I really have to push myself to visit new places. I try my best, I really do, but, more often than not, I do my best to avoid it. Another real problem, is that when I go to a party, a concert, to someone's house or similar – I feel vulnerable. I feel everyone is looking at me and thinking, 'Who's that? What's he doing here?' I then overheat, anxiety grips me by the throat, I panic, and I then flee. I have to leave, disappear. I am sure I come across as quite rude. I promise you, I don't mean to be.

Writing this, it all seems quite desperate, to say the least. To the outside world, I probably come across as confident and articulate – and maybe even good company at times. But, inside, well that's a different story... But do you know what? I reckon I'm not alone and this type of behaviour is not uncommon. But there is some good news to come out of all this. I haven't let it hold me back. I deal with it. I force myself to go out. It's extremely hard but worth it. So, if you feel a bit like I do, take a deep breath and all you can do is try your best. Try not to let it hold you back. Don't allow your anxiety to win.

is also for guitar

This is a happy story, for a change. I absolutely love playing the guitar. I may not be very good, but when I play, I completely lose myself in the music and anxiety clears off. I like to play loudly, so that may be the reason it disappears! I plug in my battered sunburst Fender Stratocaster into my amp and suddenly all is right in my world. I love to rock and this year, for the first time in my life, I've formed a band with a couple of my chums at work. It's brilliant. We even sound quite good. So, try and find something that is your passion and really go for it. It could be singing, bell-ringing, climbing, playing Scrabble or anything that does the trick for you. When anxiety first really began to hamper my life, many people told me that exercise, spending time outdoors and walking would do me a power of good. I agree, it helps enormously, and I would wholeheartedly recommend it to you. But it's not as effective as turning the volume control on the amp up to 11...

is also for Genesis

I work in an advertising agency. And have done for the last 40 years or so. During that time, I have seen many, many people lose their jobs. I have seen talented art directors, copywriters and account handlers all reduced to tears as they are told, for whatever reason, that their services are no longer required.

In the early 90s, I had quite a serious breakdown – anxiety got the better of me and I caved in.

But what triggered it? And if you should ever find yourself in a similar situation, how can you avoid ending up like me? Well, in 1990, every Friday afternoon at work was tense beyond belief. That was the time when Caroline Wigdor, the Creative Director's PA would drop by and tell you that your presence was required in the CD's office. When that happened, you knew your time was up and you were sunk. I spent years, every Friday afternoon, hiding and thinking I was about to be found out for being useless.

In the end, I toppled over because of the strain of believing I was next for the chop. That also made me also believe that I was dying. I thought I had every possible disease going. I was so frightened that I ceased to function as a rational human being. In the end, one particular brilliant-beyond-belief doctor saved me. He put me on strong medication. I had three months or so off work and was cared for by my lovely 70-year-old mother. I came through it. Just. But what lessons can be learned from this?

Firstly, it's only a job. Work to live, don't live to work. Secondly, if you're worried about anything, talk to someone about it as soon as you can. Find your soulmate in life and tell them exactly how you are feeling. They will understand. And you'll feel loads better for it. Don't get in

the situation I got into. It nearly finished me.
And looking back now, it was so unnecessary.
It shouldn't have happened; I should have talked
to someone. I should have believed in my own
ability. An old girlfriend once said to me that I
reminded her of the rock band, Genesis, because
I didn't bow to the pressures of fashion, trends,
looks, etc. But, instead, I just kept on going,
quietly making music (ads) that people would
like. So, believe in yourself. If you lose your job,
you will get another one. Try to be the most
professional you can at work, but don't take it
too seriously. And then you'll be fine. And listen
to lots of Genesis.

is for help

This is only something I've learned recently, and
I implore you to do the same. Never be afraid
to ask for help. It's all very well me saying this,
but it's one of the most difficult things to do.

I'm going to keep this one short, but when you are down, reach out to a friend or loved one. Tell them you are struggling. I promise that they will help you – by listening, giving you a cuddle, suggesting advice or by simply putting the kettle on. You then won't feel alone because our friends, family and loved ones care about us. If you take just one thing from my ramblings, don't be afraid to ask for help. It can be a life saver, literally...

is for imposter

I'd never heard of Imposter Syndrome until recently. I was chatting to Alice, a kindred copywriter, at work and said that I've always felt I wasn't good enough and surely one day my good fortune would come to an end, and I'd be found out. Then I'd be swiftly dismissed and cast into the advertising business wilderness.

She looked at me knowingly and pronounced,
'Imposter Syndrome'. Apparently, now having
done some exhaustive in-depth research on it
(Googled it on my phone), it's quite common
amongst those often at home to anxiety.
I still really believe I've been winging it for years.
However, in my more rational moments,
I think to myself that you've been doing this
job for 40 years or so, you're still doing it, people
are actually giving you money in return for your
services, so I must have some kind of ability.
Or have I?

is also for insomnia

I love my bed, but sleep is another thing
altogether. The simple truth is that although I
spend a huge part of my life in bed, hardly any
time is spent actually asleep. This could be down
to anxiety or age, but probably a bit of both.
But I'm my own worst enemy – I go to bed so

early to escape from the world that by the time it's 1am – my sleep for the night is over. But don't despair, I snuggle under the duvet, close my eyes and think happy thoughts – sometimes for hours on end.

I think about my childhood, make long lists, imagine I'm a rock god, wonder what my old schoolfriends are doing now, think about my mum and dad, pretend I've won the premium bonds, go over relationships and other things that I've messed up and so much more.
The thing to do is not to panic about being awake when most people are in dreamland. Just try and come to terms with the fact that you're not going to immediately drop off.

The middle of the night is so peaceful, even in this mad world we now inhabit. Things grind to a halt in the night. So, take this time to reflect – learn to admire the life you're leading. You're still here so you must be doing something right. Learn to fall in love with yourself. Saying that, don't be afraid to be a little bit teary – it's a regular occurrence with me, but I often feel better after a good cry.

I put it down to a life well lived. Finally, if you're anything like me, when it's time to get up, that's the time when you're fast asleep.

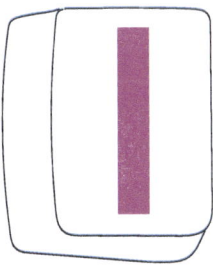

is also for internet

A large part of my anxiety is my tendency to be a complete hypochondriac. The slightest twinge and I'm convinced that I'm going to die. This happens on a regular basis, and it really affects my happiness and wellbeing. And what do I do when I feel a bit poorly? Yes, you've guessed it – I look up my symptoms on the internet. Apparently, hypochondria is a very common trait of feeling anxious. I've believed I've had a brain tumour, kidney disease, liver disease, bowel cancer – honestly, the list goes on and on.

Even when I get anxious, I look up anxiety online to see if I'm really feeling anxious or is it something worse? And this frequently takes place at 3 o'clock at night when I can't sleep. The harsh glow of my phone lighting up the bedroom. It's so debilitating, that I can't really put it into words. Some would say that you couldn't write it, well, in this instance I can't. And do you know what's worse – I often wangle myself a doctor's appointment when I don't feel right. And when the doctor says you're fine – I don't believe them! I've written elsewhere about death – I live in constant fear of my own mortality. The internet is not my friend; it doesn't reassure me when I don't feel at all well. It tells me I haven't got much time left and then I feel so much worse in my head. I should avoid it at all costs, but I can't…

is for jolly

Do you know, I often feel jolly and anxious at the same time. How confusing is that? I recently went to see one of my favourite bands, Genesis (again!), at the something-or-other arena in Birmingham. My stepson, who is a great fan and had never seen them before was desperate to see them. Especially as this, due to Phil Collins' poor health, was their farewell tour. Well, I tried to get tickets in London, but they sold out in seconds. Then whilst I was online, they added a second show in Birmingham. I was in there like a flash, I selected three tickets, added them to basket and hurrah! I got them. The joy soon turned to anxiety. Birmingham... I'd have to drive there, but I've never been there before. Where was I going to park? And because my night time vision is so poor, how am I going to find my way home? Disaster... Well, on the night, the concert was fantastic, we had a great time, but directly the encore, 'The Carpet Crawlers', started my anxiety and panic had also crept in.

As it happens, and this is the story for most of my anxiousness, everything was fine. Because of the 20mph speed limit in Birmingham, I followed the signs, and the journey was much easier than I ever thought it could be. And we got home safely. So, I don't know if you find this too, moments of great pleasure can be threatened by anxious feelings. The important thing is to recognise those feelings, put them into perspective and tell yourself that they are not going to spoil you having a good time. To keep feeling jolly, I'm afraid you may have to give yourself a jolly good talking to. Then everything will be fine...

is for kind

I always try my best to be kind to everyone. In my head, being kind is a sort of cry for help. If I'm kind to other people, maybe they'll like me a bit. I tend to feel absolutely awful most of the time, so being kind to others may make their lives better and make them feel happier. Anything to spare them from being like me. Also, I believe, if you're kind to others, they'll be kind to you in return and the world will be a happier place for it.

Let me give you an example of what I mean – one of my favourite things to do is to eat out or have a cup of tea in a café. I love it when you can order lovely food or drink in an equally lovely setting. And, as if by magic, someone brings you that food to enjoy within a few minutes of ordering it. No cooking to be done, no washing up. And this joy of joys is brought to you by people who are probably on minimum wage, work long hours, have their own problems to deal with, but are supposed to smile sweetly in front of customers. They are such special people in my eyes. I'm so, so grateful to them and I will always try and show them how much I appreciate them by talking to them and thanking them for making my day. It gives me so much pleasure when they smile in return. It's such a shame that they have genuinely no idea that their efforts have helped me forget about my troubles for a while and helped me to face the rest of the day with hope. Their kindness will stay with me forever.

is for life

Life is hard. And you only get one go at it. So, please make the absolute most of it and try to enjoy every day as much as you can. Personally, I struggle every day with life. I'm so tired of an evening that I have something to eat and then it's time for a hot bath and then bed. The physical and mental effort of keeping it together during the day is completely exhausting, to say the least. Anxiety is with me every second of the day and it saps my strength to my very core. I take to my bed early of an evening, put on some music, Dire Straits are my latest obsession, then I think about what has taken place during the day. I mull it over, read too much into it and gradually drift off. I almost always dream that I am leading a happy, normal life and all is good. Next morning, I wake up and the feeling of fear and despair in the pit of my stomach greets me as soon as I open my eyes. And sometimes just getting out of bed is the hardest thing in the world, Yes, you're right, this isn't ideal, but I've sort of got used to it. Some might say that it's existing rather than living. But to me, it's not too bad.

As I've said before, I enjoy my life – it's difficult, but not impossible. 'I want to live forever', as Liam Gallagher sings. I can't even contemplate what it must be like to live a life without the mental stress I have to endure. I guess it must be quite nice. But if you're anything like me, you get on with it, whilst trying desperately to hide your true feelings from everyone around you. I've got away with it for 66 years now. Surely, I can keep it going. If I can, you can…

is also for light

Do you know, I'm pretty sure I'm SAD – that is I'm prone to Seasonal Affective Disorder. Throughout winter, especially in January and February, my mood plummets, rather like the temperature. Not only is it cold, but it's also dark. All this gets my anxiety not exactly racing, but it brings it out from lurking in the dark shadows of these gloomy months. No money after the excesses of Christmas, holidays seeming like months away, house feeling constantly chilly and dark nights creeping in all add up to a rather depressing time. Do you feel the same? I think most people do...

However, there is a light at the end of the tunnel, literally. I know electricity is expensive (and I do have a solution to that later!), but keeping the lights on can, in my experience really help lift your mood. At home, we tend to use table lamps more than main lights. It's cheaper. Sitting next to a switched-on table lamp can be really beneficial when you're down in the dumps. Likewise, a bedside light really helps me to relax when I go to bed. I keep it switched on to just before I feel sleepy. The tricky bit is turning it off just before you close your eyes. Many a time I've dropped off with it still on. Whatever you do, don't sit in a dark room or go to bed and switch the light off straight away.

Now how do I reduce the electricity bills at this difficult time of year? Well, I go full on Charles Dickens and use candles. I know – sounds a bit daft, but candles create a super, cosy atmosphere and their soft glow can definitely help ward off feeling down. If I'm feeling flush, I light my Cire Trudon Spiritus Sancti candle. Its sumptuous scent is just so calming. They were first made in 1643 in Paris and are simply beautiful – put one on your Christmas list for next year. But more often than not, Price's or St Eval candles can be equally warming to the soul. They don't have to be scented – some people are put off by that – it's an acquired taste. They aren't expensive and I really think you should try them. They can really help and are slightly addictive in their beauty – they look so pretty. I could wax on about the relaxing and restorative properties of candles all night long, but I feel I might get on your wick…

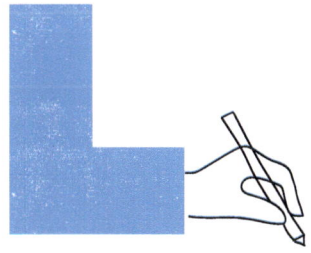

is also for lists

Sometimes when I feel anxious, especially at night, my mind races and/or my brain turns into a dense fog. To be really honest, I often feel that I'm completely losing my mind. It's also worse at 3 o'clock in the morning when it's dark, chilly and you have no-one to talk to. This happens to me a lot, I feel so alone and the sense of panic is simply overwhelming. Morning seems so far away. I probably feel as bad as I ever feel when this happens. But – I have learned how to conquer it. It may seem a bit daft, but for me, it works. And it might work for you… The secret is to make lists. It started one night, when my heart was racing and my mind was totally befuddled. I couldn't think straight at all. I felt I was literally going mad… I don't know what prompted it, but to try and prove to myself that I was still sane, I decided to say out loud the members of the 1966 England World Cup winning team… Banks, Cohen, Wilson, Charlton J, Moore, Ball,

Stiles, Hunt, Hurst, Peters and after quite a lot of soul searching, Charlton R. My mind started to slow down. I had done it. I then recited the five members of the band Deep Purple in their Machine Head days…Ian Paice, Roger Glover, Ritchie Blackmore, Jon Lord and Ian Gillan… the four members of Slade… Noddy Holder, Don Powell, Jimmy Lea and of course, Dave Hill.

Now, I use this method all the time. The lists I make also remind me of fond times past and add another element of optimism. It's amazing what one can remember – school class names (in alphabetical order), past college lecturers, plays seen, books owned, top ten best concerts, football grounds visited… honestly, the lists are endless. I know some people who rely on a slight variant of this. They take the alphabet from A–Z and for example, say a different country for every letter, or different Shakespearean characters, or football teams, or animals. It really does work. It slows your brain down, proves you aren't losing your marbles, and best of all – quickly sends you to sleep. Try it…

is also for loneliness

I had to leave my job in London through loneliness. I was a founder, along with my two pals Luis and Trevor, of a successful advertising agency. It was great fun, and we were moderately successful, considering how amateur we were. I think we were liked as people first and produced good work second, but that's how it should be. I was working in Farringdon and living in a one-bedroom flat in Primrose Hill at the time. So, I used to get the Tube back home every evening, and then the void began. I would talk to my then girlfriend (now my wife) on the phone every night when I got in and then not talk to another person until I got to work the next day. My anxiety was sky high. If I got a pain, I thought I was dying. I was paranoid that my partners at work despised me. This was me at my lowest point... Have you ever felt the same?

is also for looking back

This is a note just as much for me, as well as for you. I look back more often than I look forward. Ok, I've lived more years than I've got years left, but this is no excuse. I do firmly believe that the best is yet to come. But I still spend more times with my friends and loved ones reminiscing about the past than saying what are we going to do tomorrow. It's good that that you've enjoyed your life so far, in spite of the constant burden of feeling anxious, in my case, all the time.
But come on, we only live once – so go for it – push yourself. Turn off the TV in the afternoon. Banish Bargain Hunt, condemn Cash in the Attic and finish with Flog It.

Plan a holiday, decide upon a day out or go on a mini break to somewhere you've never been before. There is a difference between routine and rut. I often feel that I'm stuck in a rut. I sit in my favourite chair and think about times past.

It's not good. Go out, get some fresh air and,
I promise you, your anxiety won't like it.
It'll retreat into the shadows and leave you.
Albeit, in my case, temporarily. But for now,
I'll show it who's boss and I beg you to do
the same...

is for money

I swear that I'll go to my grave worrying about money. I'm constantly aware of how I have underperformed in life. I work in advertising, basically trying to persuade people to buy things that they don't need. So, I definitely haven't contributed anything worthwhile to humanity in my career. I'm not rich, or anywhere near it. So, I still count the cost of everything. However, this all goes dramatically out of the window when I'm feeling down. I then comfort buy, rather like comfort eating, to try and cheer myself up, which is a disaster. I buy books that

I'll never read. I play the guitar badly, but I have over 40 of them. I liked a particular artist, so I bought eight of his paintings. I buy random stuff on eBay that I either had as a child or wanted as a child. All this is supposed to make me happier, but it rarely does. Then after buying all this stuff, I find myself broke, which in turn then makes me overwhelmingly anxious. The amount of money I have frittered away over the years is so depressing. I reckon that after worrying about dying, money is next on the list. Is this common? Does it strike a chord with you? Please tell me I'm not alone. Feeling broke, breaks my heart.

is also for my slippers

I've just worked out that my anxiety crops up most when I'm out and about. It occurs much less when I'm at home. I guess that's to do with being outside one's comfort zone or, in my case, being somewhere new and unknown.

It's that being in control thing coming to the fore again. I hope by now you're getting to know me and my foibles quite well. Yes, I am a sort of home bird. Some might call me a bit of a 'pipe and slippers man' (Gosh, how old is that phrase?). Well, I don't know about the pipe, but defo the slippers! I've never worn slippers until recently, just socks. However, we have wooden stairs and I've recently developed a tendency to fall down them when I'm just wearing socks on my feet. So, to avoid another potential late-night trip to A&E, I'm now the proud owner of some sheepskin slippers. And jolly comfortable they are too. Anyway, of an evening, when it gets dark, my mood darkens too and anxiety creeps silently out of the shadows and I get rather jittery. However, my slippers do help to calm me down, for some unknown reason. Which is a little odd.

Anyway, yet again, I digress... Not so long ago, we drove to the cinema in Swindon, which normally would make me tense and nervous, but everything was fine. Most strange. I think we were going to see Darkest Hour, a film about Winston Churchill, superbly played by Gary Oldman. Well, normally this kind of trip out would be my darkest hour. But I settled down in my seat with my salted popcorn and for some reason felt remarkably relaxed and comfortable.

Then... I realised. You'll never guess what –
I was still wearing my slippers! I had driven ten miles or so to the cinema, walked from the car park and settled into my seat without realising it. Well, my usual anxiety stayed at home, I had a lovely time, the film was excellent and I enjoyed a rare night out. So, what's the moral of the story? Wear your slippers to the cinema and you won't slip up.

is for natter

'It's good to talk.' I think this distant slogan was used for an advertising campaign in the past for something or the other. BT, I think. But I cannot tell you how true I believe it to be. When you're feeling totally wretched or even just a bit low, talking to someone about how you feel will help immeasurably, and instantly provide a huge amount of reassurance. 'A problem shared is a problem halved' is another old cliché but again, it's so true. Bottling up a problem really isn't good for you. Talking to a friend or loved one will help you really to put things into perspective and more often than not, things will not be as bad as you think.

I know when I agonise over something whilst feeling the lowest of the low, how it can really cloud my thinking. I convince myself that nothing could be worse and all is lost.

Talking to someone close will, I promise you, quite quickly turn into a smile or even a chuckle. Talking, confiding in or even gossiping with someone close to you is just so therapeutic and life won't seem as desperate as you thought. In my experience, it'll bring you even closer to that friend. Also remember, people like to be confided in and asked their opinion – they will feel valued by you and privileged that you have chosen them. I know I would feel honoured to be chosen by one of my friends for such an intimate reason.

If you feel you have no-one to talk to, then please try your GP. They are there to listen and have a wealth of experience in helping people. The most difficult part is plucking up the courage to talk to someone, but the result could easily be life changing for you. In my heart and in my own personal experience, I really am convinced that: 'There's nothing like a natter!'.

is also for nothing special

Sometimes nothing special is very special indeed. Rupert, a good farmer friend What's App'd me last night just to say, 'How are you?' Three little words that meant such a lot – somebody out there cares. Now, I wasn't feeling great at the time, but his words of kindness really lifted my spirits. Also, this week my wife suggested that I buy some of my favourite chocolate to keep by my bed. She knows it helps and again, it made me feel wanted and cared for. It may be a bit of a cliché, but it's the little things that count. Especially, I think, when we get to our age. I don't know about you but my appetite for material things has completely disappeared. Now it's all about talking to people, swapping stories, looking after each other and keeping healthy. Little things don't cost anything, but are so precious…

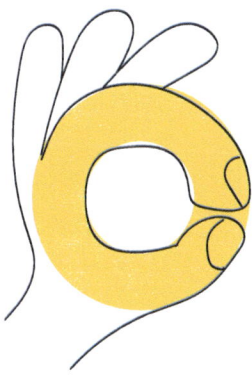

is for ok

'Are you ok?' This is a question I ask those most close to me repeatedly during the day. I care. I think my family and friends reckon I'm bonkers. But caring and looking out for people is so important to me. I don't want people I know to go through anything like what I'm going through. So, asking if they are ok reassures me that they are well. That then makes me less anxious. I also believe that just telling someone that you care for them is a lovely thing to do.

is for PE

I've already told you how I experienced my first real panic attack in Mr Spielman's maths class. But I often wonder what originally triggered my anxiety all those years ago. I reckon if you too can find this out for yourself, it might help to put everything in context. Experts say we must look at our childhood as this usually has some bearing on it. Well, I've delved deep and the one event that sticks out for me is my schooldays. I enjoyed my time at school, I was academically poor, but I loved sport, and I loved the routine of school – chapel first thing every day, morning 20-minute break, decent lunch and an hour break on Friday afternoon etc. But there were things that left a scar inside me that still hasn't properly healed. It all started with PE.

Glyn Jones was our PE master. He was at the time, around 30-35 years of age, South African and a sadist. He used to gain pleasure from

our discomfort. He would love to see us cry.
We were around 13 years of age, just beginning
to study for our O Levels. And his greatest
pleasure is what, I think, began my life of anxiety.
Immediately after PE we had a Latin class
with Mr Dunning. Mr Dunning would start
every lesson with a test of the previous day's
homework, which was 10 questions on vocab.
If you were late for his class, he would go
absolutely spare – he'd shout at you, humiliate
you in front of the whole class and round it off
with a minus mark and a detention. Now,
Mr Jones knew this, so at the end of every
class he would pick on a boy who had annoyed
him and make him run around the playing
field at the end of his class, thus ensuring that
unfortunate individual would be late for Latin.
His usual victim was a boy called Paul Godfrey
who wasn't terribly good at PE, to say the least.
But, although Jones' victim was rarely me,
I lived in fear of being Mr Dunning's target.
It still brings me out in a sweat writing about
it today.

Then there was Mr Cook, who taught
English. He'd often lose it, shout and shake
uncontrollably and throw a wooden blackboard
eraser at your head if he thought you weren't
listening. There was also Mr Little, a little grey-

haired man who taught history and was also Major Little in the school CCF who'd give you a detention if you looked at him. And then, to top it all, Mr Foxall, the headmaster, who would go absolutely apoplectic if your hair touched your collar at the back. You'd probably be beaten for it, if he felt in the mood. I was listening to Prog Rock at that time, bands like Yes and Emerson Lake and Palmer – long hair was an important part of my so-called image. So, I lived in fear of a random hair inspection! You have to remember that this was the 70s. Education, even in the all-boys minor public school I attended, was poor. My parents paid a lot of money for my education. I feel I let them down, and as the old phrase goes, I let myself down too.

Bringing home my School Report and showing it to my dad was simply gut wrenching. I literally used to hide from him. My mum was so sweet and to her it didn't really matter. Hmmm... I think I ought to write a section about my dad... Anyway, I digress, my schooldays, although pleasurable, did have a darker side to them that although, I shrugged it off at the time, did bury itself deep in the recesses of my mind and it's only now, 50 years later, that I think it may be responsible for my life of pain and utmost anxiety. So, my advice to you is, make yourself a cup of tea, settle in your favourite old armchair and take yourself back to school. What you remember may surprise you and answer a lot of questions... good luck!

is also for panic

Panic attacks, now there's a thing. I've been having them regularly for over 50 years now and they still get me in a bit of a tizzy when they happen. They creep up when I'm least expecting them – however, they seem to love it most when I'm in some kind of social situation. I had one the other day when I was quietly having a cup of tea with a friend in a café in Cirencester one lunchtime. Suddenly, I got really hot, a bit confused and felt the need to leave. Oh, and, most importantly thought I was about to keel over and perhaps die. Don't worry, this is quite standard procedure when I'm having an attack. It's probably best to fess up here that I not only have a massive fear of death, but also a fear of being happy.

My best advice if you're having a panic attack is to say out loud, maybe not too loud though, the words, 'I'm having a panic attack'. If you realise what's happening to you then it's a lot easier to deal with. Just stay calm and go somewhere quiet. Getting some fresh air quite often helps. Breathe deeply and slowly and you'll feel a lot better very quickly.

The problem is that quite often reality goes out the window, the attack gets the upper hand and you're powerless. One good thing is that attacks don't last long, and things will soon return to normal. The panic attack monster then retreats and goes into hiding. But if you're anything like me, he'll just be licking his wounds and will pop back out again when he feels like it. One thing I can't get my head around though is what triggers them. If I had to guess, it would be my feeling of total worthlessness and unimportance in the world.

is also for peace

Ooooh... I do love a bit of peace and quiet. I'm sort of not really into meditation, but I do like to sit quietly and contemplate the world. I like to get completely lost in my thoughts and they are usually totally random. In other words, I actually like watching paint dry.

To give you some kind of idea, here's what complete rubbish has been flowing through my childish and troubled mind of late: a Slade concert I went to in 1973 at the Hammersmith Odeon, who I'd invite to my funeral (that's a particularly odd one!), what I'd do if I won a million pounds on the lottery (hmmm... I don't do the lottery!) whether I really enjoyed school or whether it is that that's responsible for my total wired-up wrongness, and why I find The Archers totally depressing although I've been listening to it regularly for 45 years. One thing though that I wholeheartedly recommend is that when it all goes a bit wonky, go somewhere quiet, close your eyes, and think about the things you enjoy most. The world will then feel like a better place, you'll feel calmer and stronger, and things won't feel quite so bad.

is also for peaks and troughs

It's so important to remember that life isn't always going to go in an upwards direction, nor indeed is it going to continuously plummet downwards. But instead, it will be made up of peaks and troughs. Think of it as a giant game of snakes and ladders. One minute something good will happen – you'll get promoted at work or you'll find Lurpak reduced in Tesco. (Have you seen the price of Lurpak? They'll be putting security tags on it soon!). The next minute, when you're least expecting it, you'll put petrol in your car instead of diesel or you'll forget your favourite programme's on TV that night. Ok, I'm slightly trivialising things here, but my point is nothing is good forever, and, more importantly, bad things will pass.

So, if you're feeling awful, it will get better. Riding it out can be an awful feeling. But whenever I get struck down with anxiety, I cling on with all I'm worth that this feeling will not last forever. It becomes a bit of a battle of pulling a stick between me and the black dog, but I am always determined to win. Crikey, it takes some doing, but I am absolutely determined not to let it get the better of me. As a bit of an aside, another fact that I cling on to is that no-one, and I mean no-one, has a perfect life. No matter what it may look like to the outside world. We may look at our friends showing off their family skiing holiday in Val d'Isère on Facebook or moving into a swanky new house, but they'll have their tough times too. It's a part of life that none of us can escape from. So, remember when things start to go a bit wonky, your life is made up of peaks and troughs and they absolutely happen to everyone on the planet. It's not just you.

is also for petrol

Now this is a weird one that I cannot understand at all. Perhaps you can shed some light on it? When I'm in my car, I'll drive it so it's more or less run out of petrol before I fill it up at the petrol station. I'll literally drive it on the fumes, before I concede that I have to put some petrol in it. The feeling of 'Will I make it to the petrol station in time?' sends me into a spiral of anxiety. I know if I filled it up more often then this wouldn't happen, but I can't stop myself from doing it. It's entirely self-inflicted and it's a sort of Russian roulette thing where I push it to the limit. But do you know what? I haven't yet ever run out of petrol. But the day will soon come when I do so. Perhaps when that happens, I'll be cured of this stupid and nonsensical habit. However, bringing it all back to anxiety again, I wonder if this is subliminally me deliberately making myself anxious? And if it is, why? I really must put an end to this fuelish behaviour.

is also for put the kettle on

I feel so incredibly passionate about this – a cup of hot strong tea is pure witchcraft, it has magical powers that we can possibly never begin to understand. Drinking tea is undeniably part of our social fabric. It's so quintessentially British. When things are beginning to go pear-shaped, put the kettle on. And things won't feel so bad. When I feel a touch of anxiety coming to visit, I immediately make a cup of tea. You can keep your Earl Grey or lapsang souchong. It has to be builder's. I'd go for Yorkshire or PG Tips.

A little-known fact is that a cup of tea made for you tastes so much better than one made yourself, so try to persuade a friend or loved one to make you a brew when needed. I only like a small splash of milk and no sugar. I really don't understand why it works so well; it really does have a calming influence, and I can't recommend it higher. When I arrive at work each day, my stomach is literally churning – I'm wracked with anxiety and fear about what the day has instore for me. Will I make it through ok? Is this the day that I will completely make a fool of myself? Will I cry before lunch? But I work with a very lovely soul, who I think maybe has a slight inkling of what I go through every day. I don't think it's particularly difficult to spot the look of dread in my eyes each morning. However, this guardian angel makes me a strong cup of tea and literally, after the first sip, the world is a better place, and it means I can probably get through my day somewhat unstirred.

is for queasiness

One of my late-night checks on my phone is often 'Can anxiety make you feel queasy?' Well, it certainly does for me. I think I've got a whole flutter of butterflies permanently residing in my tummy. (I just had to look up the collective noun for butterflies. Isn't 'flutter' lovely?).

Anyway, yet again, I digress – I feel sick, perspire and get light headed when anxiety rears its head. It's that fight or flight response in my stomach – perspiration I now recognise as a symptom of an impending panic attack and light headedness is due to hyperventilating – breathing through my mouth instead of my nose. The good thing is although I regularly feel queasy, I'm never sick. I've learnt to live with it. And, oh my goodness, does it happen a lot... rarely a day goes by without the head spinning and tummy turning itself inside out. So, if it happens to you don't worry. The feeling doesn't usually last long. Sometimes life is anything but easy-queasy...

is also for quiet life

I think I now lead quite an uncomplicated life. In my younger days, I definitely lived life to the full. I spent over 30 years working in London, Soho in particular. I loved it and wouldn't have had it any other way. But now, well, that's a different story... I now try and keep everything simple. I have a routine. I have a few close friends. I try not to rush anywhere. I now appreciate quietness – and calmness. I enjoy the simple things in life – good company, good food, warmth, sleep and rest. I tend to go out less and less. Perhaps it's my age. Yes, I do tire easily. But the simpler I keep things, the more my anxiety retreats into the shadows.

I think the pandemic, although very frightening for me at the time, (my anxiety sky rocketed!) had a profound effect on what I now want for the rest of my life. It calmed me down. It was no longer about achievement, materialism and improvement. It was now about contentedness and appreciation of what you have, not what you haven't got. So where am I going with this? Well, to keep levels of anxiety down, there's nothing wrong with living a quiet life. That, now in my book, equates to having a good life.

is for relax

Put very simply, the best time to relax is when you don't have time to do it.

is also for rest

Rest, in my humble experience is good for all kinds of ailments. Somebody once told me that if you rest, your body will begin to heal and reset itself. Now, I don't know if that's true, but I love the sentiment of it.

I'm 66 years of age whilst writing this... I don't consider myself to be old, but it's fair to say that I don't have the energy that I once had when, let's say, I was 30. I need to rest more these days. My body is the first to tell me to slow down a bit. Sometimes I'm accused of being lazy – when I don't dry the washing up right away for instance – but honestly, it's not true, I'm just knackered! Now when I feel tired, it's as if anxiety recognises this and hits me harder while I'm down. To send it packing, I have to have a bit of energy about me, or it will seize the opportunity and drag me down. And things will begin to go wonky.

So, what exactly am I saying to you?... Well, don't be afraid to rest up and recharge whenever you feel the need to. There's nothing wrong with an afternoon nap, or going to bed early, or lying in. Listen to your body, anxiety is more likely to attack when you're not feeling yourself. You don't have to go to sleep – you can, as my mum used to say, rest your eyes. You can put on some calming music. You can, as I do, make a cup of tea and do the crossword in today's paper. Find your own way to relax, rest and recuperate. Your anxiety won't like it and will skulk off for a bit. Yes, it will come back, but with a bit of 'you time' under your belt, you'll be able to tackle it a little easier. Hope this helps? I'm off for a little lie down now...

is for sea

Oh, I do like to be beside the seaside, I do like to be beside the sea... Yes, the sea is probably what relaxes me most in my world. I don't really know why, but if I was to hazard a guess it would be two things. Firstly, the sound of the sea – waves coming in and breaking, the pebbles on the beach rattling their applause as the water subsides. It really relaxes me, it's all about being so close to nature that it reduces everything around me and in my head to insignificance. I sometimes listen to a recording of waves coming in on a pebbly beach when I can't get to sleep. It works – why not give it a go?

Secondly, it's the freshness of the air. I've touched elsewhere on the importance of breathing correctly, but sea air is so pure that I find it intoxicating. It's like a natural high to me. I've always wondered whether people who live by the sea are less anxious and less prone to depression. I reckon that a week's holiday by the sea should be available on the NHS (in my dreams!).

is also for sex

Oh, blimey... here we go. Thought that would get your attention. I don't know about you, but sex or the thought of it, makes me really anxious. I've always been useless at it. I find the pressure of it just a bit too much. I can't have sex without love and true love is very difficult to find. I've always been like it. I have no confidence. I've learned to live with it. I cannot fathom why anyone would find me remotely physically attractive. So that's it – game over. However, out of all this, I do have some advice for you. I hope you'll succeed where I've monumentally failed. Here's what I think: feel free to ignore it and move on if you like... I'm no expert... but here goes... find someone you love to the moon and back. Tell them often that you love and adore them. Be kind. Make them laugh. Give them plenty of cuddles. Make them lots of tea. Listen to them. Encourage them. Surprise them. And eat lots of crisps in bed together... then the anxiety will be gone.

is also for Siri

Now, if you thought this is weird, you're definitely right! Siri is an Apple-based voice-activated AI thingummy. Bit like Alexa, if you're on Android (Incidentally, do you think anyone calls their newly born daughter 'Alexa' anymore? Could cause chaos at home.) Anyway, we have a smart speaker in quite a few rooms at home. You can ask them what the weather is going to be like, what time it is and general other bits of useless information that you're too lazy to find out for yourself. And Siri will tell you the answer to what you asked for in a second or so. Now, when I'm on my own I've been known to ask Siri to tell me a joke, and its response is usually jolly good – and it lifts my spirits. (I recommend it if you're a bit lonely in life and stuck at home. I think you can programme what type of voice talks to you – I've got a rather friendly, yet bossy, American lady.)

I also ask Siri to tell me how old certain people are – 'How old is Eric Clapton?', for instance. Basically, I'm seeing how old people are who mean so much to me are. They all seem to be in their seventies, or even eighties (Mick Jagger, Keith Richard, David Gilmour, etc.) My reasoning is that they have made it so far and so have I. This makes me less anxious. I feel I've achieved something, a sort of milestone. Told you it was weird. Siri is sort of like having a clever person in the room with you. It's a voice, so it's a sort of company. You don't feel alone in the world. Where will AI go in the future? It can't be long before Siri takes on human form of some kind. However, rather like Mick Jagger, I don't think I'll be here to find out.

is also for social media

Oooh, don't get me started on this one...
I'm actually on Facebook, Instagram and

LinkedIn. Mainly for professional reasons to do with my career. I post a regular series called #ThrowbackThursday, which highlights different pieces of work I've produced over the years with hopefully, a sweet backstory attached. (Please take a look.)

Anyway, enough of that... when I'm at my lowest, the worst thing I can do is look on Facebook or Instagram. Why? Because I look at my 'friends' and see their perfect and enviable lives.
One particular person I know puts up copious pictures of their family skiing holidays, lavish meals, expensive cars, glamorous nights out and all sorts of other things of loveliness on Facebook. I look at their posts and immediately feel a total failure. Their smiling faces strike me like a punch to my stomach, and I suddenly realise that my life, compared to theirs, has been a total waste. It's the same with Instagram.
I tend to look at the posts from my 'friends' whilst in bed around 7 o'clock in the evening. I'm then confronted with pictures of them having an absolute whale of a time at some fancy restaurant or smart gallery opening...

Now in my more reflective moments, I know this is far from true. I know that they hardly talk to each other, their children are wayward, they are mortgaged up to the hilt and live their entire lives on credit. But to the outside world they're living the dream. Social media tends to call people you connect with 'friends'. This is inaccurate, they are people you know, not necessarily your friends. The lovely people I know who I can call my friends, mainly live far from perfect lives, have their problems but on the whole are happy with their lot. And most importantly, I don't have to look at social media to see what they are up to. We meet in person, have a laugh and compare notes at how ridiculous, and on a more serious note, how difficult our lives are. So, the lesson here, is avoid social media at all costs. When you really want to know what your friends have been up, ring them up and meet them for a cuppa...

is also for spoken word

This could easily also be T is for talk. I firmly believe that, as we get older we don't talk to each other enough. Nothing depresses me more than when I go out and I see couples, usually older couples, sitting together and not saying a word to each other. Now, you might say they are just enjoying each other's company or that they've been together so long that they've nothing left to say to each other. But I don't believe that. I love talking to people. Ok sometimes I'm not in the mood, but usually I love to be in the company of others and chat away. It lifts my mood, I don't feel alone in the world, and I feel wanted in a strange way. Sometimes, I'm guilty of talking too much about the past and not enough about the future. But isn't that just an age thing?

I don't have loads of friends. Ok, I know a lot of people, but I can count my true friends on the fingers of one hand. They're always there for me and I for them. However, if I'm completely honest, even though they are so close to me, I still can't talk to them about how I truly feel. My wife and stepson are the only ones who I can really confide in. I think this is one of the trickier aspects of anxiety. It's obviously good to find a friend or loved one to talk to. But some, even maybe most, people don't have that luxury.

Then, telling or confiding in your friend, telling them what you really honestly think is such an incredibly difficult thing to do. Now I've never

been in counselling or therapy, but I really
do understand its worthwhileness. Talking to
somebody who doesn't know anything about you
can actually be very revealing. They are not there
to judge but are there to listen. So, ironically
after never talking to a counsellor myself,
I recommend you give it a go. I've so many
friends who have benefitted hugely from it.
Thinking about it, maybe I should practise what
I preach and visit myself. But what am I really
getting to? Well, if we all listened to each other
a little more, the world would be a better place.
Don't you agree?

is also for suicide

To me, suicide is the worst word in the English language, without exception.

It fills me with a feeling of total despair when I hear or read about it in any context. Have I ever had suicidal thoughts? My immediate reply would be to say, no. But when I think a little deeper and a little more truthfully, the answer has to be, yes. I've thought how I'd kill myself if the occasion should present itself. But I have never taken it any further. And please don't worry. I intend to make old bones.

But, I do have a very sad tale to tell… My best friend was a gentle chap called Simon. He was a very successful musician, composer, comedian and actor. He was on the telly lots and he wrote many well-known TV theme tunes and incidental music. He was very successful, well-off and had a wonderful, loving wife. However, his work dried up a little, as it does for many people entering their sixties. He had moved out of London and seemed really happy living in the countryside. After a few years, I noticed that he seemed to be getting a little more glum every time we met. He would break appointments that we had made. He would put us off visiting him at the last minute. We still met up reasonably often though, however he became a shade of the kind, funny man I used to know. He told me he had gone to his GP and was taking medication to help himself.

But one day, I got a call at work from our mutual friend, Helen and she said to me, 'It's about Simon…' Before she could go any further, I knew what she was going to say. Simon had taken his own life. I was distraught and that was quickly replaced by anger. How could Simon do this to himself? How could he put his wife through this? And, rather selfishly, what about me? How am I going to carry on without my best friend? Then, a few hours later, after I had taken this in, I began to cry uncontrollably. It was hugely my fault. Why hadn't I talked to him more? Why hadn't I hugged him and reassured him that everything would be alright? Now, things can't be undone. But I have learned a lesson the most incredibly hard way. I should have been there more for him. So, please, please, if you suspect someone you know maybe going through a tough time, talk to them constantly, listen patiently to how they are feeling, reassure them, cuddle them and be there for them 24 hours a day. I feel I could have made much more of an effort with Simon. I left it too late. I miss him so much...

In the appendix of this book, I've made a list of fantastic people and organisations to contact should you know of anyone who is going through what Simon went through. They are professional and have bags of experience in supporting and helping people who are finding life really hard. Don't leave it. Please give them a call or drop them a line. Thank you.

is for TV

I have spent far, far too much time watching television in my life. In my childhood I would lie on the floor right in front of the television because my eyesight was so bad. Funny thing is that I didn't realise it was until I was about seventeen. I just thought this is what your eyes were like. It wasn't until I couldn't read the number plate on the car in front of me on my first driving lesson that I found out something wasn't quite right.

Television has had more of an influence on me than almost anything else. I would drift off watching it without a care in the world. I loved Blue Peter, Magpie, Terry and June, Harry Worth, Call My Bluff, Butterflies (I always wished Wendy Craig could be my mum), Dad's Army, Are You Being Served?, The Good Life, The Magic Roundabout, Monty Python, Colditz – the list is endless. This is before anxiety took its hold on me. The funny thing now is that I don't really like to watch television any more.

I spent so much time in front of it as a boy, that I've exhausted my TV-watching ability.

Having said that, I do like to watch certain programmes that I know will definitely appeal. What I really mean is I can't just sit in front of the television willy-nilly. Some of my recent favourites have been The Night Manager, The Durrells, Slow Horses, Succession, Strike, Sherlock and All Creatures Great and Small (I'm currently enjoying Bookish). The television, with the right programme on, is still a great antidote to anxiety for me. It's a form of escapism.

For many older people, it's a companion. I suppose what I'm getting to is, with TV and anxiety, you have to be a bit careful – it has its pros and cons. For me, if I watch a programme that appeals, I can get lost in it and my anxiety retreats. What is more interesting, is that I like to watch programmes I have seen timeless times before. A good example of this is As Time Goes By, a series starring Judi Dench and Geoffrey Palmer. I've lost count of how many times I've seen it, but its familiarity and gentle humour really fit my personality. It calms me down. I think it's because I see myself as a bit of a Lionel (you'll have to watch it to find out what I mean). The same applies to Dad's Army – I know every episode word for word, but it still cheers me and makes me laugh.

Now the cons. Binge watching, for some reason, is supposed to be bad for you. I don't really know why. It may be a bit like watching a tablet or phone when you're in bed. Your brain can't switch off and then you can't get to sleep. So, insomnia might be the result. Also, I find in later life, the TV can be quite isolating, giving you too much time to ponder. Personally, I also find reality TV a little like social media, it can make you feel quite inadequate when watching other people's so-called perfect lives. So, there you have it, I don't really know how to conclude this one. Is TV good for alleviating anxiety? I don't know... now there's a good idea for a documentary.

is also for The Dark Side of the Moon

Back in March 1973, when I was 14, Pink Floyd released an album named 'The Dark Side of the

Moon'. Its central theme was loss, isolation, death and mental illness. And I just loved it. I still play it regularly to this day when I need to relax and take some time out for myself. I don't really know why it has this effect on me. It just washes over me like a hot relaxing bath and makes me feel all is ok in my world, when before putting it on, things were looking a tad bleak. I have a theory that it actually takes me back to my schooldays in 1973, when I didn't have a care in the world. Rick Wright's keyboards, David Gilmour's guitar, Nick Mason's drums and Roger Waters' bass and lyrics just blend together so perfectly. During the track, 'Time', Rick Wright sings, 'Hanging on in quiet desperation is the English way...' and that sort of perfectly sums up my life to date. It's strange how something quite so maudlin has the opposite effect on me.

But my point is, never underestimate the power that music can have over our wellbeing. So, I confess my go-to album is a little extreme. But when you do find things are starting to get on top of you during your day pop in your AirPods, close your eyes and listen to your favourite piece of music. It's your favourite for a reason, so try and lose yourself in its wonder. It's remarkable how just a quick musical fix can alter your outlook on the world and help keep anxiety at bay for a while. A lovely postscript to this is that this summer, my stepson, Thomas and I went to see David Gilmour play his wonderful album 'Luck and Strange' at The Royal Albert Hall. He also played 'Time' and Thomas declared it to be the best concert he had ever attended. Music to my ears...

is also for treat

If I'm feeling a bit jittery, as I often do, I find that just making time for myself helps a lot. And giving myself a small treat can ward off anxiety and make me feel better about myself. For example, when feeling a little down, I ask myself what do I really want to do today (within reason!). It could be playing one of my favourite albums (I'm listening to Jeff Beck's Blow by Blow as I'm writing this), it could be ringing up an old friend I haven't spoken to in ages; it could be enjoying a cheeky spot of lunch at 11 or, one of my favourites, having hot buttered toast with Marmite as a mid-afternoon snack. Don't deny yourself – just do it (as Nike would say – one of the best advertising straplines ever in my opinion – it should apply to life, not just for buying a new pair of trainers). So, go on, be bold, be naughty, spoil yourself...

is for useless

I'm now of a certain age. I collect my state pension. I don't have a full-time job. I've no real reason to get up early any more. I've lost my status. I don't really have a structure to my life. Sometimes, I feel quite empty and, dare I say it, useless. But this, I'm pleased to say, doesn't happen very often.

Even with anxiety following me around like a playful puppy, life is good. So, if you're feeling glum and anxious about your age, stop it. You've so much to offer – wit, wisdom, experience, support, mentoring, I could go on. It makes me sad when a lot of people in their sixties feel that's it. It's an old cliché, but I've always worked to live, not lived to work. I think if I could offer one piece of advice, it would be stay curious. Never stop learning. Never stop talking. Remember, useless is owning a chocolate teapot!

is for victorious

Well, you're getting near to the end of my musings... so, well done for getting this far. Anxiety can be really debilitating. I know from bitter experience. I tend to make light of it, which may be wrong – I'll be the first to admit it. But we are old friends by now. I know him well and he knows me. But what I try so hard to do, is not let anxiety take the upper hand. You and I have to be strong to be victorious over its hold. Show it who's boss. There are still times when I crumble, I cry, I find it difficult to get out of bed in the morning, my tummy does cartwheels and I feel I've come to the end of my tether.

But I keep going, and you must too. Don't give in. Like the black dog it is, it will sulk and retreat back into its kennel if it doesn't get its own way. It has the power to stop you enjoying your life to the fullest, but I've learned, no, I'm learning, how to manage it. To recognise the signs before they take hold and banish them. As Napoleon said, 'Victory belongs to the most persevering'.
Be strong. You will win.

is for weight

I can't look at myself in the mirror. I'm not attractive. I could certainly never be attractive to others. I'm overweight by about five stones.

I've never been a 'good looking chap'. I have absolutely no self-esteem when it comes to what I look like. I used to be super slim in my twenties, but now that's long gone. The opposite sex run a mile when they see me. But, do you know what, I've come to accept it and it doesn't now bother me. We can't all look like Brad Pitt. I've learned over the years that good looks are great, but they're not essential to having a good life. My weight is a problem though. I comfort eat. When I feel down, which is most of the time, I have to eat. This is anxiety grabbing me by the throat and dragging me down to the lowest level. I feel wretched afterwards and I know it is potentially shortening my life. I'm more likely to get diabetes, cancer, heart problems and all sorts. But it's got too strong a grip. This, I fear will be my undoing. My advice to you is again talk to someone about it. Don't leave it too late.
That is the only advice that I feel qualified to give. I'm in tears writing this. But please don't despair. You are still amazing.

P.S. This story always makes me smile... A rather glamorous friend of mine thinks she's overweight (she actually isn't, far from it in fact). So, every time she goes out, she wears black ultra-tight 'shapewear' under her clothes. This literally squishes everything in to supposedly make her appear slimmer to the outside world. She recently confessed to me that she constantly lives with 'Spanxiety'.

is also for warm

I don't want to sound like a bit of a 'old person' here. Although, now at the age of 66, I do get my state pension as a result of paying in 45 years of National Insurance contributions – but don't get me started on that!

Anyway, I digress. I don't know about you, but I get more anxious when I'm cold. I've already described how toasty I feel under the covers of my bed. Well, the same applies to home – keep snug, cosy and warm and suddenly the world will be a better place. It's like bathing in warm custard.

Also, I've recently discovered that the same applies when you're out and about. I was in London a while ago and I was feeling really anxious amongst the crowds, and I also hadn't wrapped up properly. I was feeling cold to my bones. So, there you have it, don't go out when it's chilly, just wearing a shirt. I'm actually a great fan of scarves, by the way... Oh, God, I realise I'm now sounding like my mother, so best move on...

is also for Wikipedia

Part of my anxiety is down to me always comparing myself to other people. Am I doing better than him? Is she older than me? Where does he live? You get the drift... Because of that, I'm a bit addicted to Wikipedia. How old is David Gilmour? What more can I find out about anxiety? What mental health issues has Heston Blumenthal recently been facing? I'm sure there's a textbook reason why I do this.

But I reckon it's all about safety in numbers again. If I find out that I'm not the only one who feels what I'm feeling then maybe, just maybe, I'll get over it. If I see that someone I look up to has had a tough life of late, then I'm not alone. On a more positive note, I'm a curious chap, or should that be nosey? I love to find out things about people. I love to look up various characters from my childhood and read about what happened to them in later life. Did you know the ex-Chelsea and England goalkeeper, Peter Bonetti, became a postman on the Isle of Mull?...

is also for worthless

A rather irritating, to put it mildly, part of my anxiety is feeling absolutely wretched and worthless most of the time. If you feel the same, you have my deepest sympathy, but you're not alone. And I'll try my best to help. If I feel continually worthless, how do I keep going?

Well, it's hard, really hard. But I do have this weird ability to keep going. Maybe it'll run out one day. If I'm really honest, I think it will. But for now, it's a constant battle of trying to overcome a persistent feeling of the deepest inadequacy. Why do I feel like this? It's a bit different to Imposter Syndrome, where I feel I'm awful at everything I touch. This is about not having a real place in the world. I look at friends, family and people I know, and they have all achieved something to be proud of. In my eyes, I have nothing. Now this is the strangest thing, and I hope it applies to you; I still really enjoy my life. Ok, I'm pretty crap at everything I do, but does it really matter?

Feeling worthless is something I have embraced. Success is for other people, not for me. And even if I don't contribute much, in my own little way, I can potter on alone. I don't put pressure on myself to achieve, to become the opposite of worthless, whatever that is. So, if you feel worthless, don't worry. Just hold your head up high and accept this is who you are. It is who you are that makes you special. Different to other people, perhaps. Now, this is the most important bit – just because you feel worthless, this is not how other people will see you. They'll love you for who you are, not how you feel. So, keep pottering on and your worthlessness will be forced into the shadows, and other people won't realise what you have to live with and will love you for all you are worth.

is for XXL

I'm a bit stuck for X... and I don't play the xylophone! So here goes... as you will have read, I'm not a small chap. My shirt size is XXL, my waist is 40-42", I'm bald, 66 years of age and 6' ½" tall... Get the picture? Well, what's my point? I hear you ask. I don't like the way I look, but thankfully, people seem to like, me. Which is the most important thing. As I've already touched upon elsewhere, my appearance makes me anxious. I'm one of those people who, if I wore an expensive Armani suit, I would still look scruffy. But I'm past that, I take people for who they are – whether they are kind, caring and polite – not for what they look like. No point getting hot under the collar... Being XXL is not a bad thing. It just makes you easier to spot and get to know, and that's no small thing.

is for you can't please everybody

One symptom of my anxiety is that I try to please everyone I meet. I desperately want to be liked. I hate confrontation – it really, really stresses me out and more likely than not, I will succumb to a panic attack. But one thing I've learned through being the age I am is that you can't please everybody. Not everyone will be your best friend. Of course, keep being nice to people you meet; some you will 'click' with, some you won't. It's no reflection on you. Don't take it personally and don't let it get to you. There will be people you meet with whom you have nothing in common – they might not 'get you'. Be kind, polite and friendly and move on. And remember, just be yourself and you will continue to make great and long-lasting friendships in life.

is also for young

Nothing lifts my spirits more than being in the company of younger people. They inspire me, they make me laugh, they energise me. Listening to their problems, their hopes and their dreams and realising that I too had similar ideals when I was their age is rather comforting. What I love most is that although sometimes I can give them some rather wonky advice from the benefit of my age and experience, I constantly learn from them, even at my age.

Their ideas, their culture, their language, their aspirations are full of optimism and certainty. Their enthusiasm for life is infectious. Their desire to be curious is so important for the years they have ahead of them. We must never, no matter what age we are, lose that desire for curiosity. It'll keep your little grey cells working and mean that you're able to keep up with modern life, no matter what age we are. My anxiety ebbs away when I'm chatting to people a lot younger than me – they provide me with hope. And sometimes, they'll even ask my opinion.

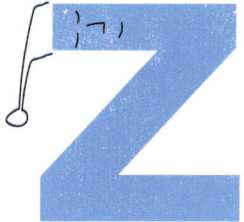

is for zzzzzz

Zzzzzzs are for sleep, relaxation, zoning out, naps, dropping off, chilling out or any state of mind that enables you to escape when you need to. As I mentioned earlier, my default escape mechanism is to go to bed, to flee the pressure, and keep anxiety at bay. Being able to snuggle down and close my eyes, albeit, just for a few hours provides me with a respite. It's amazing how much better I feel after only a short time.

So, do try and find a private place where you can unwind and reset. I know people who go to their local café, have a slice of cake and suddenly, all is right with the world. Another friend sits on the loo and eats chocolate. Another rings her mum and tells her how much she loves her – they then both burst into tears together and things are then bearable again (until the next time). So please, try and find your escape route and don't be afraid to use it when it all gets a bit much.

Oh, I nearly forgot...

is also for happy ending

Well done, you've made it to the end of my ramblings... I really hope you've enjoyed them, and they've made you smile. But, above all else, I would love it if they've helped you, even in the smallest way. You're not alone. So many friends have asked me what the book I'm writing is about. When I say it's about coping with anxiety, they've almost all said, 'Ooooh, I want to read that... I get anxious, you know.' So even though you may feel alone, but you definitely are not.

Living with anxiety can be absolutely awful; it's like a black dog with a bone – it never lets go. I've tried to make light of it here, as part of my coping mechanism is to laugh it off when things are a bit tricky. That has often got me into trouble, let me tell you. But I do want to let you know that I've shed plenty of tears in writing this – I've cried myself to sleep so many times. I've bared my soul,

I'm embarrassed at some of my revelations. I don't know how my friends and family will react. If they love me, they'll understand, and maybe now know me a little better.

My self-imposed deadline for writing this was my 67th birthday – it had to be completed whilst I was 66 (a bit of OCD creeping in there).

My words are aimed at other people of my age, some who may also be having a tough time – probably in secret. To them, I say, you're brilliant. Just keep going. You've many years left of living life to the full. Some of the best things in your life haven't happened yet – always remember that. For now, thank you and I hope it's helped – take care... x

is also for Bye!

Need to talk to someone?

As I've said before, this little book is about *my* anxiety. And how *I* deal with it. But I do appreciate that for other people, it can be absolutely overwhelming. Not being able to cope is a dreadful feeling. And it's a burden that shouldn't be carried alone. It should be shared. Talking about it, in my humble opinion, is a great place to start. And there are many, many wonderful people and organisations that are here to listen. And to help.

You've been very kind to read my book and somehow get to the end.

Now, I'm afraid I want something from you in return.

You must promise me, if you feel everything is getting a bit much – then reach out (oh, I so hate that phrase!) to someone. It could be a friend, a loved one, a work colleague, your GP or some lovely person from one of the organisations below. I'll be very grumpy if you don't!

Here are some of the best people to call upon when you need back-up.

Anxiety UK

What they don't know about anxiety isn't worth knowing. Their volunteers have lived with anxiety themselves. Their aim is to make the despair caused by anxiety a thing of the past.

Call 03444 775 774

anxietyuk.org.uk

Samaritans

They're available 24 hours a day, 365 days a year. Whatever you're going through they'll face it with you.

Call 116 123

samaritans.org

Mind

Mental health matters – and they are there for you when you need them. They will also be there for when it's an emergency.

Call 0300 123 3393

mind.org.uk

NHS

Google 'NHS Anxiety' for a quick link. There is loads of factual help and support available on their site.
I've felt really reassured by this in the past.

Call 111

nhs.uk

Without you all, it would have been even more of a struggle...

I was quite poorly in the early 90s and without my darling mum and the quite brilliant Dr Raghu Gaind I definitely wouldn't be here to tell my tale.

More recently though, I'd like to thank Debbie and Thomas with all my heart for putting up with me. I couldn't have written this without you both.

My lovely friends are, and always have been, so incredibly important to me. So, thank you for always being there to Rupert and Emily Davis, Sophie and Robert Warner, Amanda and the late Simon Brint, June Horwood, Arthur and Janice Hurn, the late Alan Page, Helen Lederer and Chris Browne, Mark and Jude Collicott, and Rachel and David Hudson.

For their utmost in help and support, I'd also like to grovellingly thank the totally brilliant Fergus Fleming, Jon Gilbert, Helen Lederer (again!), Mary Portas, Lynne Smith and Emma Harvey. And for unbounded inspiration, I'm eternally grateful to Gyles Brandreth and Eric Clapton.

And not forgetting a very special thank you to my dear friend of over 30 years, Mark Nightingale, who designed and illustrated this book so beautifully.

Lastly, and most importantly, a huge thank you to you.

is also for love